This is a piglet

with a nose called a snout

Pigs have curly tails

TED 1

and love mud

The Mummy pig is called a sow

TED 1

and she has lots of piglets in a litter

The Daddy pig is called a boar

TED 1

This is a duckling

Ducklings hatch from an egg

TED 1

and are very fluffy

This is the duckling's beak

Wings help ducks to fly

Ducks have webbed feet

which help them swim

The Mummy is called a duck

Can you count how many ducklings she has?
1 - 2 - 3 - 4 - 5 - 6 - 7

This is a calf

Here is one that has just been born

The Mummy is called a cow

She can have one calf

or two calves

The Daddy is called a bull

TED 1

This is a lamb

The Mummy sheep
is called a ewe

TED 1

She can have one

two

or even three lambs

Lambs love the sunshine

TED 1

and skipping and playing in the fields

Colour in the baby animals

TED 1